Also by Sean Covey

The 7 Habits of Highly Effective Teens

The 7 Habits of Highly Effective Teens Workbook

Daily Reflections for Highly Effective Teens

The 7 Habits of Highly Effective Teens Audio

THE 7 Habits Journal

for Teens

Sean Covey

A Fireside Book
Published by Simon & Schuster
NEW YORK LONDON TORONTO SYDNEY

FIRESIDE
Rockefeller Center
1230 Avenue of the Americas
New York, NY 10020

For information regarding special discounts for bulk purchases,
please contact Simon & Schuster Special Sales:
1-800-456-6798 or business@simonandschuster.com

Designed by Joy O'Meara Battista

10   9   8

Library of Congress Cataloging-in-Publication Data is available.

ISBN-13: 978-1-5011-0075-8

Introduction

As a teenager, I got strength from writing in my journal. This was one of my ways of renewing myself, although I didn't think of it that way at the time. Like getting into nature, keeping a journal can do wonders for your soul. It can become your solace, your best friend, the only place where you can fully express yourself no matter how angry, happy, scared, love-crazy, insecure, or confused you feel.

Just like a car, you too need regular tune-ups and oil changes. Writing in a journal is like a personal tune-up and oil change. You get in touch with your inner self; you have the ability to look at yourself and change what you don't like. Writing down your deepest thoughts and emotions can clear your mind, boost your confidence, and help you find yourself.

There is no correct way to keep a journal. Feel free to paste in mementos, ticket stubs, love notes, and anything else that will preserve a memory. My old journals are full of secrets, poor art, and bad poetry. I know a young woman who writes down daily just one thing she is grateful for that particular day. It helps her to keep in touch with what is important.

So take time to start journaling here and now. You need time out to rejuvenate the best thing you've got going for yourself—you! You need time to relax and unstring your bow, time to treat yourself to a little tender loving care. This is what this journal is all about—YOU! Happy journaling!

—Sean Covey

The 7 Habits of Highly Effective People™

1 *Be Proactive.*™ You are responsible for your life. Decide what you should do and get on with it. Don't blame others or the circumstances.

2 *Begin with the End in Mind.*™ Think of how you want to be remembered at your funeral. Use this as a basis for your everyday behavior.

3 *Put First Things First.*™ Devote more time to what's important but not necessarily urgent.

4 *Think Win-Win.*™ Have an abundance mentality. Seek solutions that benefit all parties.

5 *Seek First to Understand. Then to Be Understood.*™ Don't dive into a conversation. Listen until you truly understand the other person.

6 *Synergize.*™ Find ways to cooperate with everyone. Value the differences between people.

7 *Sharpen the Saw.*™ Continually exercise and renew four elements of your self: physical, mental, emotional/social, and spiritual.

The quotes on the following pages are taken from *The 7 Habits of Highly Effective Teens.*

THE 7 Habits Journal
for Teens

Keeping a journal will strengthen your tool of self-awareness. It's fun and enlightening to read past entries and realize how much you've grown, how stupid and immature you were with some boy or girl. Reading back through a journal gives insight into our behavior and development.

A journal is just a formal name for putting your thoughts down on paper. There are other names and forms. Some people write notes to themselves, others keep a "gratitude book."

Ask any successful person and most will tell you that they had a person who believed in them . . . a teacher, a friend, a parent, a guardian, a sister, a grandmother. It takes only one person, and it doesn't really matter who it is.

Some of the more popular life-centers for teens include Friends,
Stuff, Enemies, Self, and Work. They each have their good points,
but they are all incomplete in one way or another, and they'll mess
you up if you center your life on any one of them to the exclusion of
the others.

I read a saying once that says it better than I can: "If who I am is what I have and what I have is lost, then who am I?"

Principles will never fail you. They will never talk behind your back. They don't get up and move. They don't suffer career-ending injuries. They don't play favorites based on skin color, gender, wealth, or body features. A principle-centered life is simply the most stable, immovable, unshakable foundation you can build upon, and we all need one of those.

The next time you look in the mirror, say something positive about yourself.

Renew yourself. You've got to take time for yourself, to renew and to relax. If you don't, you'll lose your zest for life.

Try to go an entire day without negative self-talk. Each time you catch yourself putting yourself down, you have to replace it with three positive thoughts about yourself.

There are two types of people in this world, the proactive and the re-active—those who take responsibility for their lives and those who blame; those who make it happen and those who get happened to.

Proactive people make choices based on values. They *think* before they act. They recognize they can't control everything that happens to them, but they can control *what they do about it.*

The fact is, we can't control everything that happens to us. We can't control the color of our skin, who will win the NBA finals, where we were born, who our parents are, how much tuition will be next fall, or how others might treat us. But there is one thing we *can* control: *how we respond to what happens to us.* And that is what counts! This is why we need to stop worrying about things we can't control and start worrying about things we *can*.

Life often deals us a bad hand and it is up to us to control how we respond. Every time we have a setback, it's an opportunity for us to turn it into a triumph.

You have the power within you to rise above whatever has been passed down to you. No matter how bad your predicament is, you can become a change agent and create a new life for yourself.

Some people mistake a can-do attitude for being pushy, aggressive, or obnoxious. Wrong. Can-do is courageous, persistent, and smart. Others think can-do people stretch the rules and make their own laws. Not so. Can-do thinkers are creative, enterprising, and extremely resourceful.

Do something today that you have wanted to do but never dared. Leave your comfort zone and go for it. Ask someone out on a date, raise your hand in class, or join a team.

By saying "Begin with the end in mind," I'm not talking about deciding every little detail of your future, like choosing your career or deciding who you'll marry. I'm simply talking about thinking beyond today and deciding where you want to take your life, so that each step you take is always in the right direction.

_____

_____

_____

_____

_____

_____

_____

_____

_____

_____

_____

_____

_____

_____

_____

_____

_____

_____

Why is it so important to have an end in mind? I'll give you two good reasons. The first is that you are at a critical crossroads in life, and the paths you choose now can affect you forever. The second is that if you don't decide your own future, someone else will do it for you.

Without an end of our own in mind we are often so quick to follow anyone who is willing to lead, even into things that won't get us far.

So, why not write your own personal mission statement? Many teens have. Mission statements come in all types. Some are long, some are short. Some are poems and some are songs. Some teens have used their favorite quote as a mission statement. Others have used a picture or a photograph.

For an on-line tool to help you create your own mission statement, go to www.franklincovey.com/missionbuilder/index.html

It's been said, "A goal not written is only a wish." There are no ifs, ands, or buts about it, a written goal carries ten times the power.

Life is a mission, not a career. A career is a profession. A mission is a cause. A career asks, "What's in it for me?" A mission asks, "How can I make a difference?"

Life is a mission, not a career. A career is a profession. A mission is a cause. A career asks, "What's in it for me?" A mission asks, "How can I make a difference?"

Ask yourself, "Would I want to marry someone like me?" If not, work to develop the qualities you're lacking.

One of the few things that can't be recycled is wasted time. So make sure you treasure each moment. In the words of Queen Elizabeth I on her deathbed: "All my possessions for one moment of time."

It takes guts to stay true to your first things, like your values and standards, when the pressure is on. Staying true to your first things will often cause you to stretch outside your comfort zone.

Never let your fears make your decisions. You make them.

One way I've learned to overcome fear is to keep this thought always in the back of my mind: *Winning is nothing more than rising each time you fall.*

If your self-confidence and self-respect are low, how can you expect to have the strength to resist? Make a promise to yourself and keep it. Help somebody in need. Develop a talent. Renew yourself. Eventually you'll have sufficient strength to forge your own path instead of following the beaten ones.

Are you a pleaser, someone who says yes to everything and everyone? If so, have the courage to say no when it's the right thing to do.

_____

_____

_____

_____

_____

_____

_____

_____

_____

_____

_____

_____

_____

_____

_____

_____

_____

_____

_____

_____

_____

_____

One of my favorite quotes is "On their deathbed nobody has ever wished they had spent more time at the office." I've often asked myself, "What do they wish they had spent more time doing?" I think the answer might be "Spent more time with the people they love." You see, it's all about relationships, the stuff that life is made of.

Have you ever had a day where everything is going wrong and you feel totally depressed . . . and then suddenly, out of nowhere, someone says something nice to you and it turns your whole day around? Sometimes the smallest things—a hello, a kind note, a smile, a compliment, a hug—can make such a big difference. If you want to build friendships, try doing the little things, because in relationships the little things *are* the big things.

"**O**ne kind word can warm three winter months."
—JAPANESE SAYING

*S*trong minds talk about ideas; weak minds talk about people.

The next time a group starts gossiping about another person, refuse to participate in the gossip or stick up for that person. You can do so without sounding self-righteous.

Pick one important relationship in your life that is damaged. It may be with a parent or a sibling or a friend. Now commit yourself to rebuilding that relationship one deposit at a time. Remember, it may take months to build up what took months to tear down. But little by little, deposit by deposit, they'll begin to see that you are genuine.

Before you go to bed tonight, write a simple note of apology to someone you may have offended.

Try to go one whole day saying only positive things about others.

Comparing yourself to others can become an addiction as strong as drugs or alcohol. You don't have to look like or dress like a model to be good enough. You know what really matters. Don't get caught up in the game and worry so much about being popular during your teen years, because most of life comes after.

Keeping a journal can do wonders for your soul. It can become your solace, your best friend, the only place where you can fully express yourself no matter how angry, happy, scared, love-crazed, insecure, or confused you feel. You can pour your heart out in your journal and it will just sit there and listen.

Sometimes, no matter how hard you try, you won't be able to find a win-win solution. If you can't find a solution that works for both of you, decide not to play. No Deal. If you and a friend can't agree on an activity one night, split up and get together another night. Or, on a more serious note, if you and your girlfriend or boyfriend can't develop a win-win relationship, it might be best for you to go No Deal and part ways.

Think of a person who you feel is a model of win-win. What is it about this person you admire?

Pinpoint the area of your life where you most struggle with comparisons. Perhaps it's with clothes, physical features, friends, or talents.

The deepest need of the human heart is to be understood. Everyone wants to be respected and valued for who they are—a unique, one-of-a-kind, never-to-be-cloned (at least for now) individual.

Have you ever heard the saying "People don't care how much you know until they know how much you care"? How true it is. Think about a situation when someone didn't take the time to understand or listen to you. Were you open to what they had to say?

Although we feel the impulse to give advice when someone comes to us with a problem, it is important to remember that sometimes people just want to be understood, not advised. Once people feel understood, they are more open to our advice.

Seeking first to understand requires consideration, but seeking to be understood requires courage.

Unexpressed feelings never die. They are buried alive and come forth later in uglier ways. You've got to share your feelings or they'll eat your heart out. If you have taken time to listen, your chances of being listened to are very good.

A good band is a great example of synergy. It's not just the drums or the guitar or the sax or the vocalist, it's all of them together that make up the "sound." Each band member brings his or her strengths to the table to create something better than each could alone. No instrument is more important than another, just different.

When we hear the word *diversity* we typically think of racial and gender differences. But there is so much more to it, including differences in physical features, dress, language, wealth, family, religious beliefs, lifestyle, education, interests, skills, age, and style.

Instead of trying to blend in and be like everyone else, be proud of and celebrate your unique differences and qualities. A fruit salad is delicious precisely because each fruit maintains its own flavor.

Have you ever felt stereotyped, labeled, or pre-judged by someone because your skin's the wrong color, your accent's too heavy, or you live on the wrong side of the tracks? Haven't we all, and isn't it a sick feeling?

There is no formal way to keep a journal. Feel free to paste in mementos, ticket stubs, love notes, and anything else that will preserve a memory. My old journals are full of poor art, bad poetry, and strange smells.

We aren't born with prejudices. They're learned. Kids, for instance, are color-blind. But as they mature they begin to pick up on the prejudices of others and form walls.

Brainstorm with your friends and come up with something fun, new, and different to do this weekend, instead of doing the same old thing again and again.

There are numerous ways to expand your mind. However, the best approach may simply be to *read*. As the saying goes, "reading is to the mind what exercise is to the body." Reading is the foundation of everything else and doesn't cost that much, unlike other methods, such as traveling.

Don't let school get in the way of your education. Although grades are important, becoming truly educated is more important. So make sure you don't forget why you're going to school.

You say you don't like school. I say, What does that have to do with it? Does anything good in life come easy? Does an athlete like working out every day? Does a medical student enjoy studying nonstop for four years? Since when does liking something determine whether or not you should do it? Sometimes you just have to discipline yourself to do things you don't feel like doing because of what you hope to gain from it.

Don't make long-term career decisions based on short-term emotions, like the student who chooses his or her major based on the shortest registration line. Develop a future orientation; make decisions with the end in mind.

You gotta wanna. In the end, the key to honing your mind will be your desire to learn. You've gotta really want it. You've gotta get turned on by learning. You've gotta pay the price.

As you set out each day, look for opportunities to make deposits and build lasting friendships. Listen deeply to a friend, parent, brother, or sister without expecting anything in return. Give out ten compliments today. Stick up for someone. Come home when you told your parents you'd be home.

Sex is about a whole lot more than your body. It's also about your heart. In fact, what you do about sex may affect your self-image and your relationships with others more than any other decision you make. Before you decide to have sex or to continue having it, search your heart and think about it . . . carefully.

It's too bad that as we age we tend to forget what made childhood so magical. One study showed that by the time you reach kindergarten, you laugh about three hundred times a day. In contrast, the typical adult laughs a wimpy seventeen times a day. Why are we so serious? Maybe it's because we've been taught that laughing too much is childish. We must learn to laugh again.

Laughter has also been shown to promote good health and speed healing. I've heard several accounts of people who healed themselves from serious sickness through heavy doses of laughing therapy.

Learn to laugh at yourself when strange or funny things happen to you, because they will. As someone once said, "One of the best things people can have up their sleeve is a good funny bone."

What is it that moves your soul? A great movie? A good book? Have you ever seen a movie that made you cry? What was it that got to you? Think about it.

Your soul is your center, wherein lie your deepest convictions and values. It is the source for purpose, meaning, and inner peace. Sharpening the saw in the spiritual area of life means taking time to renew and awaken that inner self.

What is your spiritual diet? Are you feeding your soul nutrients, or are you loading it with nuclear waste? What kind of media do you allow yourself to take in? Have you ever even thought about it?

You'll be amazed at the results a few small changes can bring. Gradually, you'll increase in confidence, you'll feel happier, you'll get high "naturally," your goals will become realities, your relationships will improve, and you'll feel at peace. It all begins with a single step.

Make as many friends as you can, but don't build your life on them alone. It's an unstable foundation.

Our confidence needs to come from within, not from without, from the *quality of our hearts*, not the *quantity of things* we own. After all, he who dies with the most toys . . . still dies.

We have paradigms not only about ourselves, but also about other people. And they can be way out of whack too. Seeing things from a different point of view can help us understand why other people act the way they do. We too often judge people without having all the facts.

Our paradigms are often incomplete, inaccurate, or completely messed up. Therefore, we shouldn't be so quick to judge, label, or form rigid opinions of others, or ourselves for that matter. From our limited points of view, we seldom see the whole picture or have all the facts.

Hard work is an especially important principle. There's no shortcut for hard work. You can't fake playing golf, tuning a guitar, or speaking Arabic if you haven't paid the price to get good. As the NBA great Larry Bird put it, "If you don't do your homework, you won't make your free throws."

We crawl before we walk. We learn arithmetic before algebra. We must fix ourselves before we can fix others. If you want to make a change in your life, the place to begin is with yourself, not with your parents or your boyfriend or your professor. All change begins with you. It's inside out. Not outside in.

We should treat the commitments we make to ourselves as seriously as those we make to the most important people in our lives.

If you're feeling out of control in life, focus on the single thing you can control—yourself. Make a promise to yourself and keep it. Start with real small $10 commitments that you know you can complete, like committing to eat healthier today. After you've built up some self-trust, you can then go for the more difficult $100 deposits, such as deciding to end an unhealthy relationship or not going after your sister for wearing your new clothes.

Go out of your way to say hello to the loneliest person you know. Write a thank-you note to someone who has made a difference in your life, like a friend, teacher, or coach. The next time you're at a toll-booth, pay for the car behind you. Giving gives life not only to others but also to yourself.

Be gentle with yourself. Don't expect yourself to be perfect by tomorrow morning. If you're a late bloomer, and many of us are, be patient and give yourself time to grow.

Honesty is always the best policy, even when it's not the trend.

Proactive people focus on the things they *can* control. By doing so they experience inner peace and gain more control of their lives. They learn to smile about and live with the many things they can't do anything about. They may not like them, but they know it's no use worrying.

To reach your goals in life, you must seize the initiative. If you're feeling bad about not being asked out on dates, for instance, don't just sit around and sulk. Do something about it! Find ways to meet people. Be friendly and try smiling a lot. Ask *them* out. They may not know how great you are.

Imagine an eighty-foot rope stretched out before you. Each foot represents one year of your life. Teenagehood is only seven years, such a short span of rope, but those seven affect the remaining sixty-one for good or bad, in such a powerful way.

We are free to choose our paths, but we can't choose the consequences that come with them. Have you ever gone water sliding? You can choose which slide you want to go down, but once you're sliding, you can't very well stop. You must live with the consequences . . . to the end.

_____

_____

_____

_____

_____

_____

_____

_____

_____

_____

_____

_____

_____

_____

_____

_____

_____

_____

An important part of developing a Personal Mission Statement is discovering what you're good at. Everyone has a talent, a gift, something that they do well. Some talents, like having the singing voice of an angel, attract a lot of attention. But there are many other talents, maybe not as attention-grabbing but every bit as important, if not more—things like being skilled at listening, making people laugh, forgiving, drawing, or just being nice.

Make a goal bite-sized. Instead of setting a goal to get better grades in all your classes, you might set a goal to get better grades in just two classes. Then, next semester, take another bite.

To overcome peer pressure, you've got to care more about what *you* think of you than what *your peers* think of you.

Keeping small commitments and promises is vital to building trust. You must do what you say you're going to do. If you find you can't keep a commitment for some reason (it happens), then let the other person know why.

People need to be listened to almost as much as they need food. And if you have time to feed them, you'll create some fabulous friendships.

In order to be a genuine listener you must first listen with your eyes, heart, and ears.

*S*ometimes, to hear what other people are really saying, you need to listen to what they are *not* saying.

_____

You are destined for great things. Always remember, you were born with everything you need to succeed. You don't have to look anywhere else. The power and light are in you!

If your motive for giving someone feedback isn't in the other person's best interest, then it's probably not the time or place to do it.

Nothing is wrong with enjoying your comfort zone. In fact, much of your time should be spent there. But you know that people who seldom try new things or spread their wings live safe but boring lives!

"**Y**ou miss 100 percent of the shots you never take."
—Wayne Gretzky

If you're not laughing much, what can you do to start again? I suggest developing your own "humor collection," a collection of books, cartoons, videos, ideas—whatever is funny to you. Then, whenever you're feeling down, or taking yourself way too seriously, visit your collection.

Are you familiar with the myth of the phoenix? After every life span of 500 years, the beautiful phoenix would burn itself on a pyre. Out of the ashes, it would arise, reborn. In like manner, we can regenerate ourselves out of the ashes of a bad experience. Setbacks and tragedies can often serve as a springboard for change.

There is a time for everything. A time to be balanced and a time to be imbalanced. There are times when you'll need to go without much sleep and push your body to its limit, for a day, a week, or a season. And there will be times when eating junk food out of the vending machine is your only alternative to starving. This is real life. But there are also times for renewal.

You'll accomplish more in life if you borrow strength from others. Mountain climbers "rope up": they tie themselves together with ropes to aid them in climbing and to save lives if one person were to fall. You can also "rope up" in life—with friends, brothers, sisters, girl-friends, parents, counselors, grandparents, pastors. The more ropes you have out, the greater your chances for success.

Want to be in our book?

Then tell us your story! Perhaps you have your own story of using 7 Habits principles to overcome challenges personally, in your family, with your friends, or at work or school. Or perhaps you've heard of one. Write us about those experiences and how you were motivated to succeed. If we accept your story, you'll be in our next 7 Habits for Teens book.

Send your entry to:

e-mail: 7Hteen@7Habits.com
or log on at: www.franklin covey.com

Fax: (801) 496-4225
Attn: 7Hteen

Mail:
Franklin Covey Co.
Attn: MS2233/Teen Dept.
466 West 4800 North
Provo, UT 84606-4478
USA

Be sure to make a copy, as we cannot return submissions!

CPSIA information can be obtained
at www.ICGtesting.com
Printed in the USA
BVHW072123110921
616349BV00006B/28